Endpapers: Part of a fresco painted on a wall in the tomb of Nebamun. The goldsmiths and joiners are skilled craftsmen who made precious objects for tombs, temple offerings and the palaces of kings. The treasures found in the tomb of Tutankhamen are fabulous examples of their skill.

SEE INSIDE

AN EGYPTIAN TOWN

SERIES EDITOR
R.J. UNSTEAD

WARWICK PRESS

Series Editor and Author
R. J. Unstead

Illustrations

Bill Stallion   Linden Artists
Francis Phillips   Roy Coombs

Published 1978 by Warwick Press, 730 Fifth Avenue,
New York, New York 10019

First published in Great Britain by Hutchinson
and Co. (Publishers) Ltd. in 1977

Copyright © 1977 by Grisewood and Dempsey Ltd

Printed in Great Britain by W. S. Cowell Ltd.
Ipswich, Suffolk

6 5 4 3 2 1

Library of Congress Catalog No. 77-85159

ISBN 0-531-09068-X

CONTENTS

Below: Bust of Akhenaten, the strange young king. In art, he encouraged a more realistic style; so, in statues and reliefs, he is seen to be a rather ugly man, with a big nose, thick lips and a fat belly. Left: A tomb painting of about 1400 BC from Thebes, the capital which Akhenaten abandoned.

2.26.79 Walts 5.60

Akhetaten

The city of Akhetaten stood on the east bank of the Nile about 202 miles (325 km) north of Thebes. Its building was begun in about 1375 BC at the orders of the pharaoh who came to the throne as Amenhotep the Fourth.

For many years the greatest of the Egyptian gods had been Amun or Amen, once merely the local god of Thebes, where his priests had become immensely rich and powerful. The young monarch, Amenhotep, came to believe that a god called Aten, "the disk of the sun" was not merely greater than Amen and all the other Egyptian deities but was the only god.

He commanded his astonished people to worship only Aten and, in the fourth year of his reign, decided to replace Thebes, home of Amen, by a new capital, sacred to Aten. It must be built, he declared, in a place which "belongs to no god, to no goddess, to no prince, to no princess". Having found the site, he decreed that the capital be called Akhetaten. His own name contained the hated name Amen, so he changed it to Akhenaten.

The site of the new city (known today as el-Amarna) was a D-shaped sandy plain about 6 miles (9 kms) long and 3 miles (4½ kms) wide. The straight side of the D was the Nile.

By the King's orders, hundreds of workmen, architects, and officials must have been transported to the site by boat to lay out the town and erect its buildings. Within two years it was advanced enough for Akhenaten to move there with his beautiful wife, Nefertiti, their little daughters, and all the nobles and court officials and servants. As far as we know, he never left it for a single day during the rest of his life.

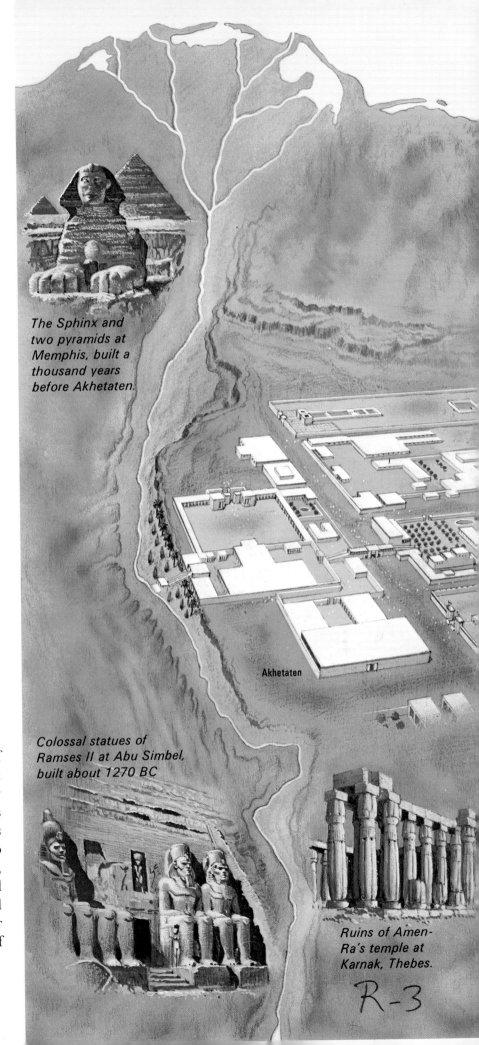

The Sphinx and two pyramids at Memphis, built a thousand years before Akhetaten.

Akhetaten

Colossal statues of Ramses II at Abu Simbel, built about 1270 BC

Ruins of Amen-Ra's temple at Karnak, Thebes.

R-3

The Streets of Akhetaten

Akhetaten occupies a narrow strip little more than half a mile (one kilometer) wide. Because the fertile strip along the river is too valuable to be built on, the city has had to be built along a strip of barren land where wells have been sunk to obtain water. There could be no question therefore of building a compact city surrounded by a wall. Instead, there are several areas of development spaced out along the strip – the Main City, with the Royal Palace and Temples, the North Suburb, South City and Palace of the Southern Pool (called Maru-Aten). There is also, strangely enough, a Workmen's Village, well inland on the desert and far from any water supply.

King's Way, the most westerly and important thoroughfare, connects Maru-Aten to the Main Center and then runs on to the most northerly tip of the city. All the main roads are wide – as much as 160 feet (50 meters) in places – and without any paving. Lesser streets connect the main roads, more or less at right angles, but there is nothing neat and regular about them. Some of them open out into a little square with a well in the middle. Even the major roads are not continuously straight, for, in places, a road has to go around a house that for some reason has been built in its path.

Right: An artist's reconstruction of ancient Akhetaten, the new capital founded by the pharaoh Akhenaten. After his death the city was abandoned and the royal court returned to Thebes, the old capital. All the houses at Akhetaten were built at ground-floor level.

The main areas and buildings in the central city, containing the temples, palaces, and government offices:

1 King's Way
2 The Great Palace
3 King's House
4 The Bridge, containing a window from which the King shows himself to his subjects.
5 Main Hall
6 Coronation Hall
7 Royal Magazines, containing the treasure.
8 Royal Temple
9 Great Temple
10 The Sanctuary
11 Slaughterhouse
12 North Suburb

THE NILE WATERWAY
The river front has quays and wharves for the unending arrival and departure of boats bringing foodstuffs, materials and merchandise of every kind. Here also land traders, artists, craftsmen, and foreign ambassadors. Across the river, a huge area of land is under cultivation.

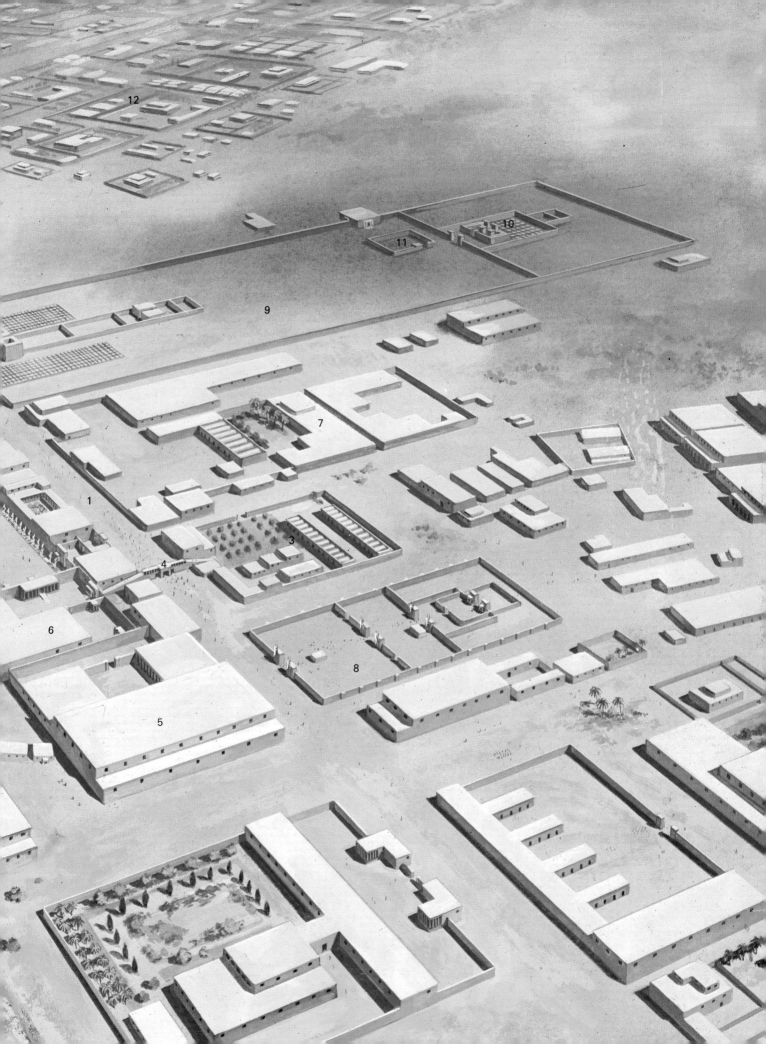

Building a House

In Akhetaten, houses are very much alike; that is, the house of one rich noble is similar to all the other houses belonging to rich nobles. The same is true of middle-class houses, and a workman's hovel is like all the other hovels.

Basically, a house consists of a main central room with smaller rooms grouped around it to keep it cool in summer and warm in winter. The main room is built higher than the other rooms, so that windows can be placed near ceiling level to let in light.

Houses of both rich and poor are made of sun-dried bricks, for the annual flooding of the Nile leaves behind vast quantities of mud, providing an unlimited supply of cheap building material. When the wet mud has been prepared, the brick-maker uses a hollow wooden mold to shape the brick, leaving it alongside rows of other bricks to dry in the hot sun.

In poor houses, the walls may be only one brick thick but, in most cases, builders lay a course at least two bricks thick, with a layer of mortar between each course. To finish off the

Builders' tools, which include a square, mallet, plumb line, dowel peg and plasterer's smoothing trowel. They are made of wood and copper, for iron is almost unknown.

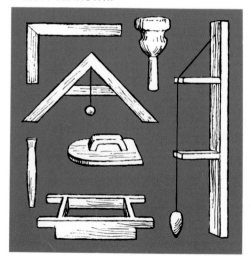

outside, walls are given a coat of mud plaster that is sometimes whitewashed but often left to dry in its natural color. Mud plaster also serves to cover the floor, on top of a layer of bricks or, in poor houses, simply on the leveled ground. Large tiles of mud are laid in some of the finer houses and painted in bright colors.

Wood is scarce and expensive, because Egypt's native trees, the palm, acacia and sycamore cannot be sawn into planks or will provide only short lengths of timber. Palm trunks can be used for posts and, sawn lengthwise, for ceiling beams, but all the other timber has to be imported, usually from Lebanon where cedar grows abundantly. Wood is therefore used sparingly; as a rule, only for columns, doors and staircase support. The wooden columns supporting the roof stand on circular limestone bases and, in better houses, stone is used for thresholds, doorways and lintels, which are carved with the name and titles of the owner, if he is a man of importance.

These small houses, often built alongside mansions of the rich, have flat roofs with the usual light shelter providing shade. The staircase comes up from the entrance hall or kitchen. Notice the bread oven in the yard.

On the building site above, workmen are carrying water to be mixed with the mud by foot and hoe. Chopped straw is trodden in to improve the strength and binding quality. The brickmakers are said to "strike" bricks when they lay them in rows to dry for two or three days. Laborers carry finished bricks to a half-built house on slings attached to a yoke balanced on one shoulder.

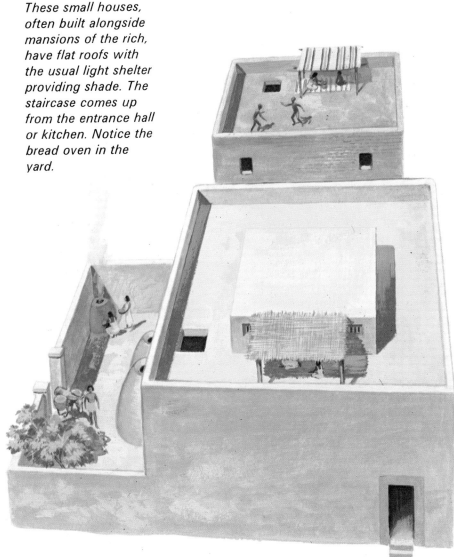

11

A Nobleman's Villa

On the King's Way, in North Suburb, stands a nobleman's residence which has become the best known house in Akhetaten. Enough of it has survived for over three thousand years to give an accurate picture of its layout and decoration. Basically it resembles nearly every other house in the town, for its main feature is a central living room surrounded by lots of other rooms.

The house stands (or rather stood, for only ruins are left) in extensive grounds, surrounded by a high wall. You enter by a towered gateway (1) and, having been checked in by a gatekeeper, whose lodge is to your left (2), you walk up a tree-lined path to the family place of worship, a little temple (3) fronted by a flight of steps and a pair of painted columns. The path turns right to lead you into an inner courtyard from which you enter the house by a flight of shallow steps. Then you pass through a doorway framed in stone, its lintel carved with the owner's name. From the porch you go through a vestibule (4) and are led by a servant into the North Loggia (5). This is a handsome reception room (loggia means a kind of porch). From here you enter the Central Hall (6), the heart of the house, (see pages 14–15).

The West Loggia (7) is mostly used as a sitting room in winter. Guest rooms are also on this side of the house. The private quarters on the other side of the hall include a sitting room for the women (8), their bedrooms and the master's bedroom (9) with his bed standing on a dais in a niche.

The bathroom (10) contains a small slab on which the master lies while a slave pours water over him. Beyond the bathroom is the toilet.

Stables (12), servants' quarters (13), kitchen (14) and cattle yard (15) are on the southern and eastern sides, because the prevailing wind will carry away the smells.

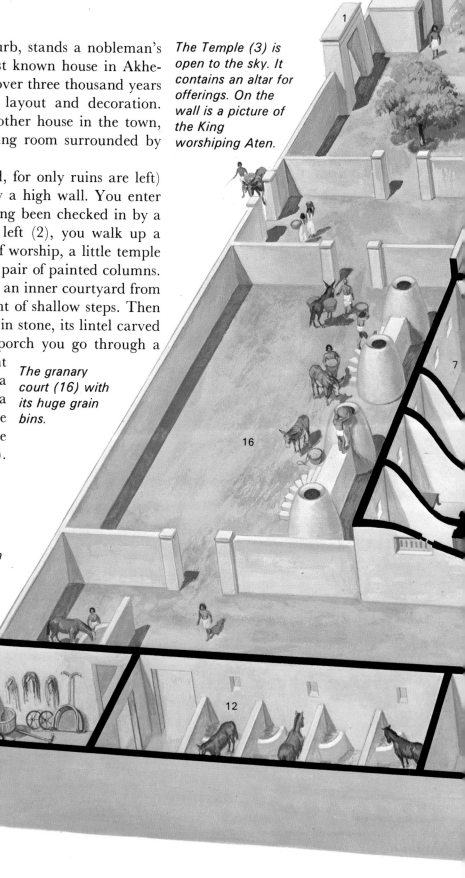

The Temple (3) is open to the sky. It contains an altar for offerings. On the wall is a picture of the King worshiping Aten.

The granary court (16) with its huge grain bins.

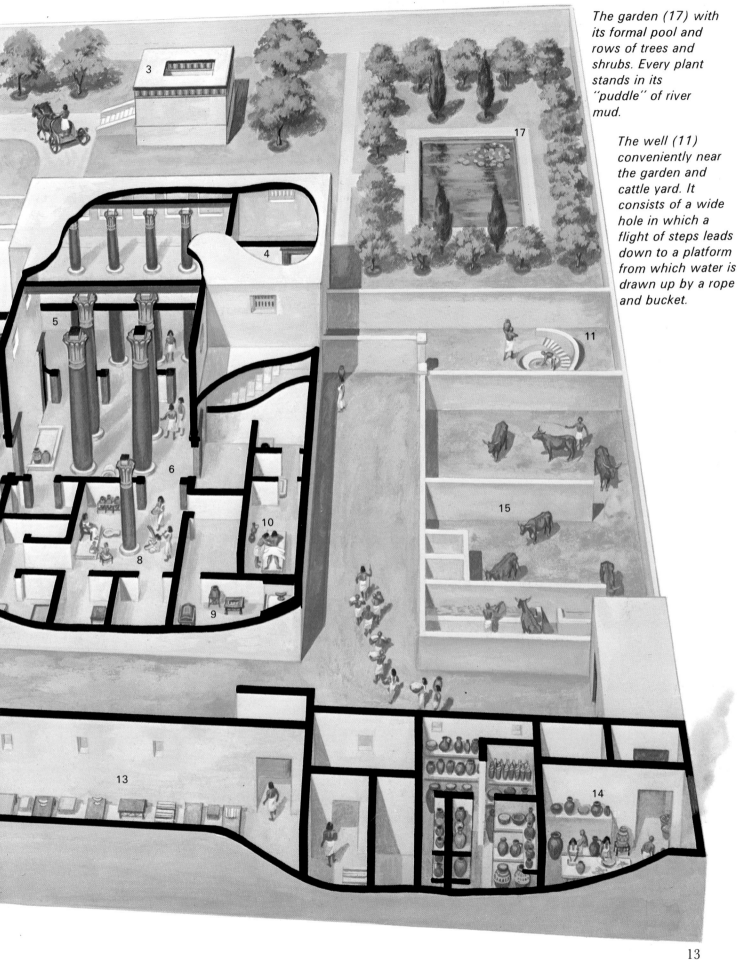

The garden (17) with its formal pool and rows of trees and shrubs. Every plant stands in its "puddle" of river mud.

The well (11) conveniently near the garden and cattle yard. It consists of a wide hole in which a flight of steps leads down to a platform from which water is drawn up by a rope and bucket.

The Central Hall

The Central Hall is the heart of a nobleman's residence. The lofty blue painted ceiling is supported by four pillars, and, high up, close to the ceiling, there are several small windows with vertical bars.

The room has two interesting features. Against one wall is a low brick dais on which the master and his principal guests sit. Next to the dais is a brick hearth on which a brazier filled with burning charcoal is placed on cool evenings. On the other side of the room is the *lustration* slab, a limestone slab with a raised edge and a runnel to carry water off into a vase standing at the side. A servant pours water from another vase over the hands and feet of a visitor who has come in from the dusty city, and dries them with a linen towel.

Notice the number of recesses or niches in the walls, gaily painted in panels of red and yellow. They are there to satisfy the Egyptians' love of balance. If a door on one side of the room is not matched by another opposite, then a niche is put there instead. Similarly, if there are real windows at the top of three sides of the walls, identical windows are painted on the fourth side.

From the Central Hall a staircase leads up to the roof, where a light shelter has been built to provide shade from the sun, and where you can get a fine view of the whole estate.

The walls of these houses are not covered with painted scenes as in the royal palaces, but are finished in soft colors. Columns are usually red and the cross-rafters pink, while the ceiling may be decorated with rosettes.

A family scene in the Central Hall of a nobleman's house. The master and his wife are seated on the left with one of their children, while two guests play a kind of checkers. Notice the pet cats, the elegant furniture, and wine jar.

TIME TO RELAX

The King's earnest interest in religion does not keep his people from enjoying themselves. They are affectionate, kindly people who love social life, music and dancing. A wealthy householder hires musicians, like the harpist in this picture, and professional dancers to entertain his guests at parties and banquets. Some people place a cone on their head made of scented pomade which melts in the warm air and drenches the hair with sweet-smelling ointment. It is customary for young children to go naked, while maid-servants and slaves normally wear only a girdle or a loincloth.

The Great Temple

The greatest and most important building in the city is the Great Temple of Aten, the center of worship of the new god. It stands in a huge rectangular enclosure or *timenos*, some 870 yards (800 meters) long and 330 yards (300 meters) wide, surrounded by a high boundary wall. Should you be granted the privilege of entering the Temple, you do so from the west end of the enclosure. You pass between tall towers into a courtyard where you see ahead of you the massive front

Set in the north wall is a large building called the Hall of Foreign Tribute. In it, flights of steps ascend to the King's throne, set on a platform beneath a richly decorated canopy. Here Akhenaten and Nefertiti receive gifts and taxes from visiting princes and ambassadors. Inside the walls of the enclosure is a huge slaughter yard where cattle are killed and the carcasses prepared for the offering tables.

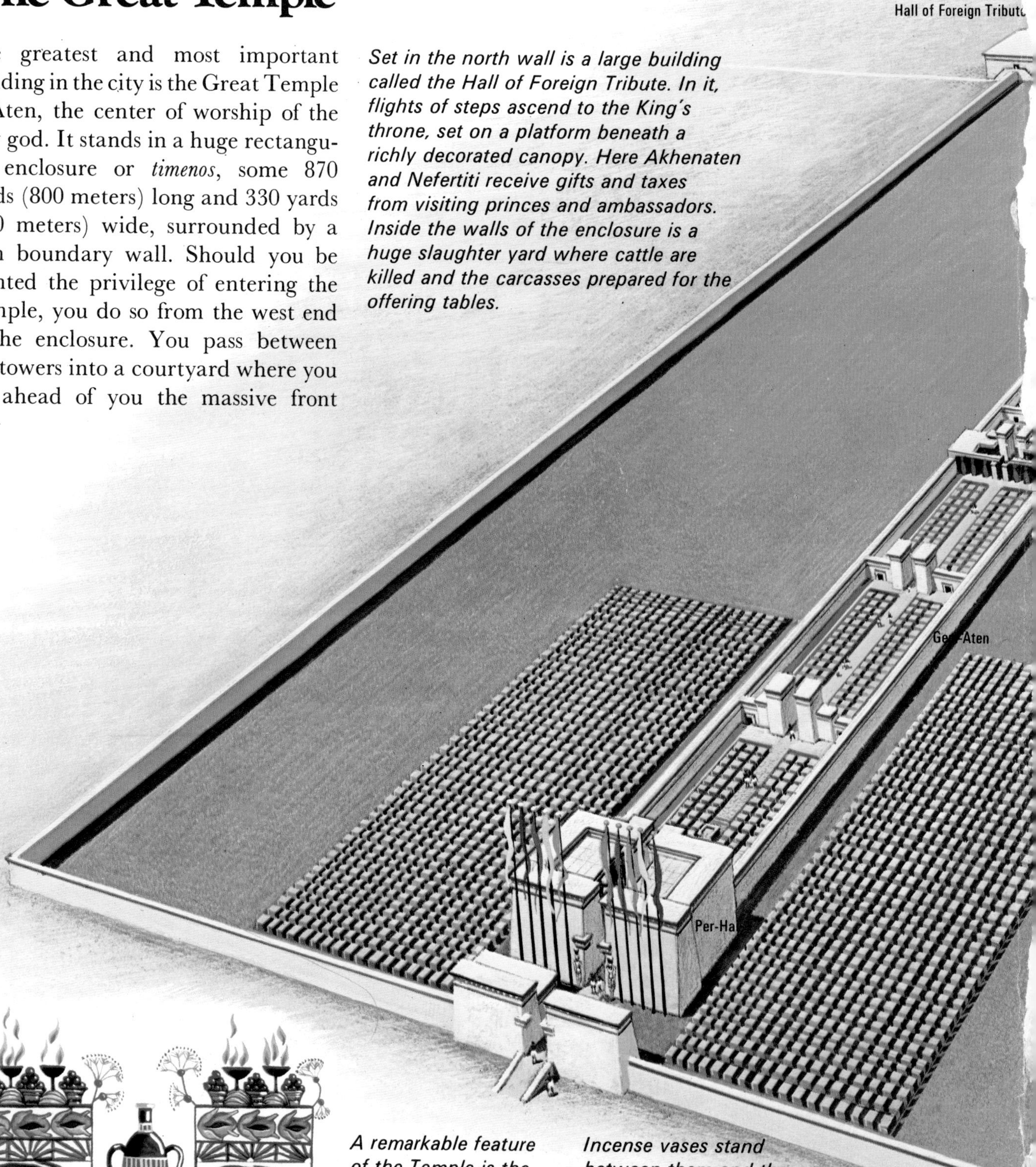

Gem-Aten

Per-Hai

A remarkable feature of the Temple is the presence on either side of the causeway of rows and rows of squat mud brick pillars. These are offering tables which are piled with fruit, flowers, vegetables and meat.

Incense vases stand between them and the chapels. Outside the walls of Per-Hai and Gem-Aten are more of these offering tables. They are for the use of ordinary persons not privileged to enter the Temple.

16

Sanctuary

Slaughter Yard

King Akhenaten and Queen Nefertiti, accompanied by a little princess, make offerings of fruit and flowers to Aten, in the Sanctuary of the Great Temple.

of Per-Hai, the House of Rejoicing. In front of its stone-faced towers stand ten immense flagpoles with fluttering pennants, and you pass through a hall filled with columns and adorned with wall-carvings of the King and Queen.

From Per-Hai, you reach the next part of the Temple, Gem-Aten – the Finding of Aten. Ahead of you stretches a long, narrow court, with an altar approached by a flight of steps. Beyond the altar is a causeway that runs toward another pair of lofty columns. This brings you into a second court, then into a third and finally into three smaller sanctuary courts. Each court leads into another, and each has its central altar and surrounding chapels. There is no exit from the eastern end, nor from the sides, so the King, Queen and priests have to return to the entrance after they have worshiped at the High Altar of the farthest court.

At the eastern end of the Temple enclosure stands the Sanctuary. Here we enter a walled court and pass between towers into a second court dominated by huge columns and four colossal statues of King Akhenaten. Walls block the view ahead, but a passage leads into the heart of the Sanctuary, the Holy of Holies, with the High Altar and surrounding chapels all open to the sky.

When you enter an Egyptian temple to a god such as Amen, Ptah or Horus, you go from the sunshine into a gloomy colonnade. Then you enter a dim hall and, as the floor rises and the roof lowers, you are in the darkness of the Sanctuary. In this awesome atmosphere, priests wash, anoint, clothe, feed and worship the god's statue every day. The Temple of Aten is quite different, for he is the god of sunshine and light, so the courts are open to the sky and worship takes place to the accompaniment of music and singing.

The Fruits of the Nile

The *Cultivation* is the name given to the fairly narrow strip of land on both sides of the Nile. There it is possible to grow crops because once a year the river rises and spills over, depositing fertile soil along its banks.

At Akhetaten, the fertile land on the east (or city) bank is used mainly for pleasure gardens. Farming, to produce food for the city population and offerings for the temple, takes place on the west bank.

Here, you can see a busy scene at harvest time. Workers are cutting the grain near the top of the stems. Others load the ripe ears into baskets which are carried to the threshing floor. Cattle are treading out the grain, as men fork away the spent ears. Nearby, the mixed grain and chaff are tossed into the air with wooden winnowing fans so that the wind carries the chaff away. The clean grain is placed in baskets whose numbers are noted down by a scribe.

The peasants who work the royal lands on the west bank live over there in villages of small huts. They probably never visit the new city on the other side of the Nile.

In the picture, there are also gardens in which general crops are grown, some beehive shaped granaries and a herd of goats. Boats, laden with produce, are crossing the river to the city wharves. The farming year begins in November, when the *inundation* or annual flooding has ended. Harvesting takes place in spring and finishes by May. Principal crops are *emmer* (a kind of wheat) and barley, used mostly for making beer, the chief drink of the Egyptians. Flax is grown for making linen which everyone needs, since it is almost the only material used for clothes.

Gardens, which have to be watered regularly from ditches and pools, produce fruit and vegetables, such as beans, lettuce, lentils, onions, leeks, melons, gourds, figs, and pomegranates.

OFFERINGS FOR ATEN

Much care is taken in growing masses of flowers for the temple of Aten. Animals and birds are reared not only for food but also for religious sacrifices. Oxen and sheep are more valuable than pigs and goats, while donkeys are the beasts of burden. The finest cattle are raised in the Delta, but there is enough grazing for small herds near the villages of Upper Egypt. Geese are kept for the table and for sacrifice, as well as ducks and pigeons.

The Pharaoh's Pleasure Garden

The Great Palace in the main city is not the King's only residence. About a mile south of the city stands Maru-Aten, the Palace of the Southern Pool. It consists of two oblong enclosures, the smaller one containing a handsome pavilion · with a great columned hall and a throne room. In the grounds is a small lake surrounded by trees. A gate leads through the wall into a larger enclosure almost filled by a shallow lake. A stone pier runs out into the water with steps at the end from which guests can go aboard the pleasure boats. In the garden stands another pavilion where the King may choose to rest and perhaps entertain his courtiers, for it contains two wine cellars. There is also a chapel and a water garden or aquarium with tanks for fish or water plants. Behind a screen wall stand the little houses of workmen who look after this estate.

North of the Temple stands the Northern Palace which has been built to cater for the King's love of nature. It contains a garden, with enclosures for cattle and antelope, a lake and aviaries where Akhenaten spends hours watching the rare and beautiful birds.

Servants set the table with fruit, flowers and wine for the royal picnic.

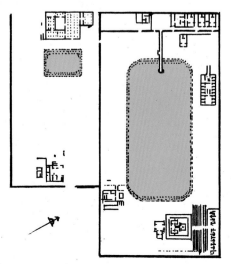

Plan of the enclosures at Maru-Aten, the Palace of the Summer Pool.

Queen Nefertiti, Akhenaten's beautiful wife, with their three little daughters whom they love dearly.

King Akhenaten in a pensive mood. He is a poet who composes hymns to Aten, the sun god.

A girl harpist and a fan bearer, a slave from Nubia, part of the Empire lying south of Egypt.

The Workmen's Village

In the desert to the east of the city is a hollow in which lies a walled village. This is a curious spot for any kind of habitation, since it is far from the river and from any well or canal. Every drop of water, as well as all stores, has to be transported by donkey.

The village itself is equally strange, for it consists of 73 small houses, all exactly the same size and of almost identical layout. There is one larger house belonging to the overseer. The houses are built in terraces separated by five narrow streets, and the whole prison-like compound is surrounded by a strong wall in which there is only one gate.

It is clear that the villagers *are* prisoners, for guards patrol the roads running along the surrounding hills.

The wall seems intended, not to keep an enemy out, but to keep the inhabitants in. They are, in fact, tomb workers, brought here to excavate and decorate the tombs in the nearby cliffs. This work fills ordinary citizens with dread, so that it is carried out by slaves, criminals and violent characters who are best confined to this walled enclosure far from the civilized life of Aten's city.

Each cottage, five yards wide where it fronts on to the street and ten yards deep, contains four rooms – an entrance hall, living room, bedroom, and kitchen. A staircase, usually in the hall, leads up to the roof on which there is generally a shelter made of matting and poles. Here and there a householder has built a little room on the roof with mud brick walls. The entrance hall has a window close under the roof and the living room, built higher than the other rooms, has windows looking over the flat roof.

The villagers make no attempt to decorate the outside of their mud brick houses, but indoors, the rooms are usually whitewashed or decorated with frescoes of flower patterns. There are even human figures, painted with materials the workmen bring home from the tomb chapels.

Some of the villagers have built a manger against the house wall for a cow or donkey.

The entrance hall (1) contains the workman's tools, the weaving loom and often a manger for the family goat.

The living room (2) contains a low brick dais covered with mats and cushions, the great round-bottomed water jar and stools. There is a hearth for a charcoal fire and, at night, the room is lit by lamps consisting of saucers with a flickering wick floating in oil.

The kitchen (3) is furnished with a brick bread oven, shaped like a big pot, bins and baskets for grain and other food, and sundry bowls and cooking pots.

Rock Tombs

In the rocky cliffs which lie east of the city, the King has presented his leading officials with sites for their tombs. These have been excavated by gangs from the Workmen's Village. Aten may have taken the place of all the other gods, but Egyptians still believe in a life after death and in the importance of a tomb which preserves a dead man's body, with scenes showing how he has served the King in this life.

Quarriers cut into the cliff to make a corridor, which becomes T-shaped when a cross corridor is cut at the farther end. A burial chamber (1) contains a deep shaft grave and, beyond the cross corridor, lies the shrine with a statue of the dead man (2). The roof is held up by columns shaped and decorated to resemble papyrus stalks. The tomb walls are smoothed so that they can be covered with pictures and scenes created by the sculptors and painters.

All the tombs contain sculptures glorifying the King. We see him, usually accompanied by the Queen, making offerings to Aten, or arriving in his chariot at the Temple, or rewarding his loyal servants with gold necklaces which he places around their necks. We also see details of everyday life – single-masted cargo ships, for instance, at their river moorings, peasants with cattle and donkeys, and criminals caught by the police and being handed over to the city officials.

Work is going on at several tombs at the same time. They belong to such important people as Huya, the Royal Chamberlain, Penthu, the King's Physician, Nay, Bearer of the Fan, and Mahu, Chief of Police.

Between the Workmen's Village and the cliffs are some tomb chapels (below) built of mud brick. Each contains a brilliantly decorated shrine in which offerings of food and drink will be placed for the middle class owner who is to be buried in one of the shaft graves.

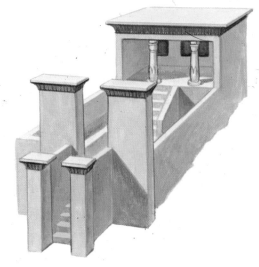

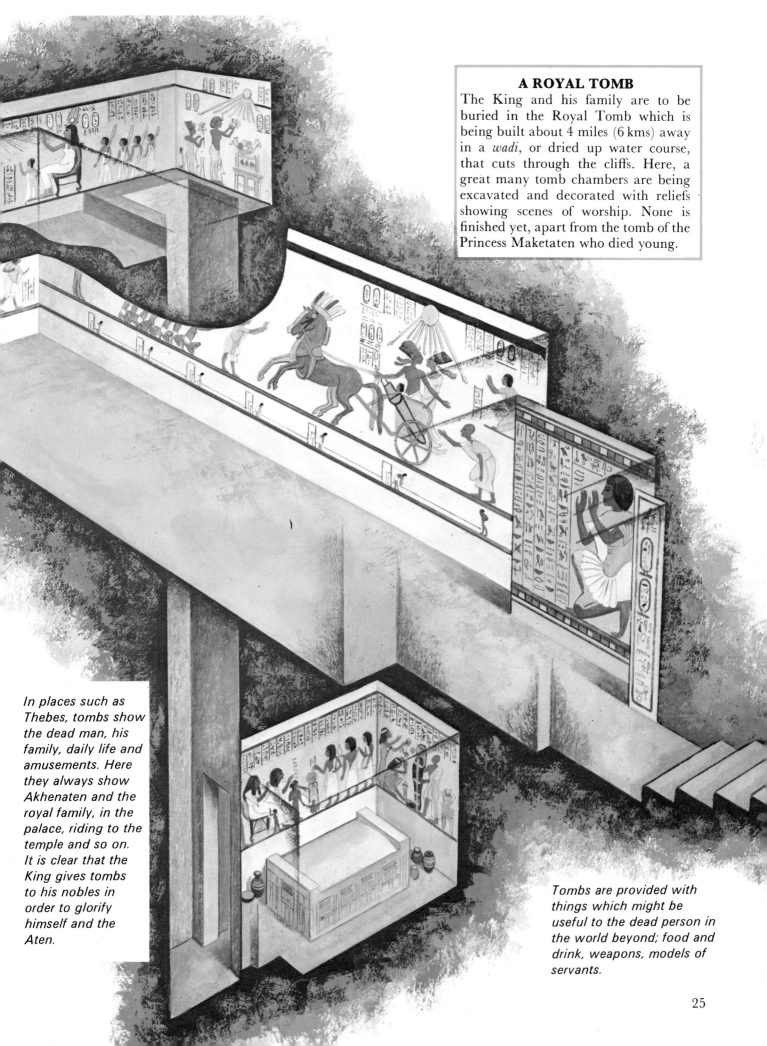

A ROYAL TOMB

The King and his family are to be buried in the Royal Tomb which is being built about 4 miles (6 kms) away in a *wadi*, or dried up water course, that cuts through the cliffs. Here, a great many tomb chambers are being excavated and decorated with reliefs showing scenes of worship. None is finished yet, apart from the tomb of the Princess Maketaten who died young.

In places such as Thebes, tombs show the dead man, his family, daily life and amusements. Here they always show Akhenaten and the royal family, in the palace, riding to the temple and so on. It is clear that the King gives tombs to his nobles in order to glorify himself and the Aten.

Tombs are provided with things which might be useful to the dead person in the world beyond; food and drink, weapons, models of servants.

25

The End of the Story

The death mask made of beaten gold inlaid with semi-precious stones which covered the face of Tutankhamen's mummy. It is of the finest workmanship and is a realistic portrait of the young King.

Tutankhamen the harpooner stands on a raft ready to throw his harpoon at Seth, who is transformed into a hippopotamus.

Akhenaten's dream city was inhabited for only a few years. Built at tremendous speed, it was abandoned even more quickly after the "heretic" King's death.

Things had been going wrong for some time before that. The cost of the new capital and the King's neglect of his duties were causing unrest.

Perhaps Akhenaten decided to take some action. Perhaps Queen Nefertiti, devoted to the new religion, opposed him. We cannot be sure, but it seems that a terrible quarrel resulted in Nefertiti's disgrace and retirement to a palace in the north end of the city, probably with the young prince Tutankhaten. Two years later, Akhenaten died and Tutankhaten, aged nine, was proclaimed King. Probably because of his mother's influence, he was not made to return to Thebes immediately, but when she died in about the third year of the reign, the priests of Amen had their way. The King changed his name to Tutankhamen and was received in Thebes with great rejoicing. Not long afterward he was to be buried amid fabulous riches.

Akhetaten had been abandoned. And, a few years later, a king named Horemheb decided to wipe out every trace of the heretic city. Temples, palaces and mansions were razed to the ground, the tombs were desecrated and the name of Akhenaten hacked out wherever it occurred. For centuries, the city's very existence was forgotten until, in 1887, a peasant woman unearthed some clay tablets which proved to be letters sent to Akhenaten's court. Excavation of the site began in 1891 and, although it has never been completed, enough has been discovered to enable us to picture the city that flourished so briefly 3000 years ago.

Gods of Ancient Egypt

There were hundreds of gods, many of them local deities, from which some emerged as national gods. Many were shown with human bodies and animal or other shaped heads. Here are a few of them:

AMEN, also Amun, the great god of Thebes.

ANUBIS, the jackal god of the dead and of embalmers.

ATEN, god of the sun-disk.

BAST, cat goddess of the Delta.

BES, the dwarf with a lion's face, god of music, jollity, home.

GEB, god of the earth, husband of Nut.

HAPY, the Nile god, shown as a man with heavy breasts.

HATHOR, cow-headed goddess of happiness, wife of Horus.

HORUS, falcon-headed sky god, son of Osiris and Isis, avenger of his father. The king became Horus during his life on earth.

ISIS, mother goddess, wife of Osiris.

KHNUM, the ram-headed god, who made man on a potter's wheel.

KHONS, the moon god.

MAAT, goddess of truth, bearing an ostrich feather on her head.

MIN, god of fertility.

NUT, the sky goddess whose curved body formed the arch of heaven.

OSIRIS, god of the underworld and of the Inundation: husband of Isis; the King after death.

PTAH, principal god of Memphis, patron of craftsmen.

RA or RE, sun god of Heliopolis.

SETH, god of violence, murderer of Osiris his brother.

THOERIS, hippopotamus goddess, patron of women in childbirth.

THOTH, ibis-headed god of writing; scribe of the gods.

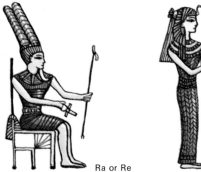    

Ra or Re   Isis   Osiris   Anubis   Horus

GLOSSARY OF TERMS

ANKH the cross-like symbol of life, often carried by gods

CARTOUCHE an oval shape, containing the King's name in hieroglyphs

CLERESTORY windows set between the top of walls and the roof to let light into central halls

COLOSSUS a huge statue of a god or king

DEMOTIC a kind of writing, more advanced than hieroglyphs, used for everyday business

DYNASTY a family of rulers, making a division or period of Egyptian history

HIERATIC a development of hieroglyphic writing in which scribes used signs rather than pictures

HYPOSTYLE hall of a temple whose roof was supported by many columns

KA the spirit of a man which lived on after death and for whom offerings of food and drink were placed in the tomb

MUMMY a body (from which internal organs were removed) treated with natron and ointments and wrapped in bandages to preserve it from decay

NATRON a form of soda using in embalming

PAPYRUS tall plant with feathery head, used to make rope, baskets, boats, sandals and paper

PHARAOH meaning royal palace, came to be applied to the King

PYLONS the great twin towers at the entrance to a temple

SARCOPHAGUS casing for a coffin made of wood, stone or gold

STELA a stone slab or pillar with carvings; used as marker-post, tombstone etc.

The double crown of the kings of Upper and Lower Egypt.

The three great Pyramids of Giza are over four thousand years old and were counted among the Seven Wonders of the World in ancient times. The largest and oldest one, the Great Pyramid of Khufu (Cheops), contains about 2,300,000 blocks of stone, each weighing about two and a half tons.

IMPORTANT HAPPENINGS

Note. Historians do not always agree on dates of events in Ancient Egypt. The spelling and form of some names vary, e.g. — Amenhotep — Amenophis; Amen — Amun; Thotmes — Tuthmosis.

c. 3100 BC Union of Upper and Lower Egypt by Menes. Capital at Memphis. Copper tools, large-scale irrigation.

c. 2686–2181 BC The Old Kingdom Pyramid Age: great pyramids and Sphinx built. Rise of Heliopolis and Re, the sun god. Principal kings were Djoser, Cheops, Khafre, Pepi II. Wars with Libyans and Nubians. Timber imported, copper mined, stone used for building and sculpture. Rise of feudal nobles led to decay of royal power.

c. 2181–2050 1st Intermediate Period Disorder; break-up of united kingdom; pyramids robbed.

c. 2050–1786 The Middle Kingdom Egypt reunited under Mentuhotep II. Thebes the capital; rise of the god Amen. Colossal temples and statues built. Nobles suppressed; Nubia conquered. Increase in wealth, culture, art.

c. 1786–1567 Second Intermediate Period Invasion of Hyksos from Asia. Nubia and Lower Sudan regained freedom. Introduction of horse chariots, bronze, improved weaving.

c. 1567–1085 The New Kingdom 18th Dynasty Pharaoh Ahmose I ousted the Hyksos. Under Amenhotep I, Thotmes I, III and IV, Amenhotep II, the Empire was enlarged from Nubia to the Euphrates. Queen Hatshepsut fostered trade, peace, building. Under Amenhotep III, (1420–1385 BC) Egypt reached its zenith of power and wealth. Vast temples built at Luxor. Royal tombs in the Valley of the Kings. Amenhotep IV (Akhenaten) failed to establish Aten as sole god. Tutankhamen restored power of Amen-Re and Thebes. Horemheb destroyed the city of Akhetaten (el-Amarna).

1320–1200 19th Dynasty Seti I and Ramses II maintained the Empire, fought the Hittites. Great temples built at Abydos, Karnak, Abu Simbel.

1200–1085 20th Dynasty Ramses III, last of the great Pharaohs, repelled the Libyans and Peoples of the Sea. Thereafter, military power declined, Asiatic provinces were lost, royal tombs were looted, and Egypt became lawless and impoverished.

1085–333 Late Dynastic Period Egypt again divided: Libyan and, later, Nubian pharaohs occupied the throne. Assyrians sacked Memphis and Thebes (670 BC). A period of recovery followed, with much trade in Mediterranean. 525 BC Persians conquered Egypt but were later expelled, so that the 30th Dynasty was the last native house to rule. 343 BC Persians reconquered Egypt but were defeated by Alexander the Great. After his death, one of his generals founded the Ptolemaic Dynasty which lasted until Egypt became a Roman province in 31 BC.

INDEX

Acknowledgements
Photographs: Endpapers Michael
Holford; page 6 Michael Holford
(left), Ronald Sheridan (right);
p. 26 British Museum (top), Ronald
Sheridan (bottom); p. 28 Zefa.